BOOKS BY WILL ALEXANDER

POETRY

Impulse & Nothingness (Green Integer, 2011)
Aboriginal Salt: Early Divinations (White Press Inc., 2011)
The Brimstone Boat (Rêve à Deux, 2011)
The Sri Lankan Loxodrome (New Directions, 2009)
Exobiology As Goddess (Manifest Press, 2005)
Above the Human Nerve Domain (Pavement Saw, 1998)
Asia & Haiti (Sun & Moon, 1995)
The Stratospheric Canticles (Pantograph Press, 1995)
Vertical Rainbow Climber (Jazz Press, 1987)

FICTION

Diary as Sin (Skylight Press, 2011)
Sunrise in Armageddon (Spuyten Duyvil, 2006)
Arcane Lavender Morals (Leave Books, 1994)

PHILOSOPHY

Mirach Speaks to his Grammatical Transparents (Oyster Moon Press, 2011)
Towards the Primeval Lightning Field (O Books, 1998)

ESSAYS

On the Substance of Disorder (Inset Press, 2011)
Inalienable Recognitions (eohippus labs, 2010)

DRAMA

Inside the Earthquake Palace (Chax Press, 2011)

COMPRESSION & PURITY

CITY LIGHTS SPOTLIGHT SERIES NO. 5

WILL ALEXANDER

COMPRESSION

&

PURITY

CITY LIGHTS

SAN FRANCISCO

The editor would like to thank Peter Maravelis, Nanos Valaoritis,
and Marie Wilson for their assistance with this book.

ACKNOWLEDGMENTS
Some of these poems have appeared in the following publications: *nocturnes,
580 Split, Traffic, Exquisite Corpse, Callaloo*, and *Barrow Street.*

CITY LIGHTS SPOTLIGHT
The City Lights Spotlight Series was founded in 2009,
and is edited by Garrett Caples.

Library of Congress Cataloging-in-Publication Data
Alexander, Will.
Compression & purity / Will Alexander.
p. cm. — (City lights spotlight ; no. 5)
ISBN 978-0-87286-541-9
I. Title. II. Series.
PS3551.L357716C66 2011
811'.54—dc22

2010054609

All City Lights Books are distributed to the trade by
Consortium Book Sales and Distribution: www.cbsd.com

For small press poetry titles by this author and others,
visit Small Press Distribution: www.spdbooks.com

City Lights Books are published at the City Lights Bookstore,
261 Columbus Avenue, San Francisco, CA 94133
www.citylights.com

To Leslie Scalapino

you of the symbolical hive
you of the oddness of its presence
always casting from your prisms
the aura of the oblique

CONTENTS

COMPRESSION & PURITY

THE BLOOD PENGUIN

"I am the carnivore
the hounded night walker
searching for my wings scattered under glass

they claim I should return to monomial transfixing
to exhibit A & no further

to some
I am six foot & lizard

to others
I am considered a mange lamb
returned from the tropics

I am never given due as to sum or proportion
I am seen as the source of something leprous
as no longer the motive of who I was thought I was shaped
to be

I who live as mislaid damage
as part of pointless verbal ejecta

there are no nouns to ensnare me
to fish up my blood so as to summon consensus

I am never that condition within the fire of conjoinment

I am never to be
the human boy genius
the archivist
the bartered child contending with study

I am none of the above
none of the aforesaid compendiums

I am the animist
the vertical lion tundra
the diamond bird who burrows under snow

because of my leaning
I know the stark Egyptian soma

much as would a blinded cemetery scribe

& because I understand
one's basic neural unravelment
I am seen as piacular
as specter
as both standing & freezing
being of some other form
from some other planet

as clinical moray addendum
this contains in itself
blackened scrawl marks from Moravia
from squandered quanta from the Sunda Islands
from quaking fogs from Santiago

they say I suffer from powerful deafening by resistance
my eyes wild & in-ferocious with lapses

the attention span blunted
the astrological paralysis shifted

so they say the unknown is the trigonomic
is the transcended nucleus
the born equational spell
according to the flaws in universal summoning

I am ancient pantomime who cannot grasp
who cannot transgress his inherited Landino

as to Mayan glyphs & squares
I am plummeted
I am simply without the means to conduct my own prism

to take on the culpable mean
at circumstantial limit

I exist through negated practical limit
through parallel sub-causes
without knowing the desire
to seek the enzymes of living

I am without & without & without

I who create doubt & the genetics of perpetual conflict

I could be strange as a human half wrought
who poses himself as Ilario Pozuelos

& what is claimed against me
is not unreasoned
is not the treatise of post-fanatics

instead
it is a curious treatise on circumstantial exhibit

it says
my values are possessed by distance
like someone humbled or plagued by a treaty

my dispossessed senses
described by these methods
under the forms of the treasonous

it tells me I am lifeless blood equipment
that my genes are not useful
that my mind is simply stricken or exposed

yet such a chronicle loses spores in the glaciers
it says
I am of Africa & the sea coast
of Ghana & the Seychelles
of insular breakage near the Azores

yet it states my non-placement
my cavern
my debilitating refuge

not even a dwelling beneath the stars
as etheric camp-base on Saturn

such is the ether climb
the sub-revelation as dialectical cartography
conjoining with the ocelots
swimming across the prisms of Mauritius

or simple flatland in Manchuria

these are seen as soils no known warrior can claim

because I readily announce my resistance
my tone as carnivorous psychic sparring
wandering beyond pervasive death concussives

claimed
by genetic dis-logistics
by anarchic ruin
by Jurassic sibling serosas

I cannot describe by cursory enclosure
external motivation
or any rotary or back-flowing water attainment

it is described as simulacra
as ghost data
as hibernation through pillage
non-specific
post-necrotic
partaking in part as jonquil & longevity

of course the cells blaze
infinity evolves
the monsoons project through containment

yet nothing resolves
nothing forbears & is clement

I exist
as steep electrical ice
asking of myself spells
of pointless dominating fuels

within this agnostic current
I describe
myself as one who's hellish
who's buried his weight with a double insistence
who seems to sleep in a brazen cylinder of peril

then after a pause in listening
calling myself The Blood Penguin
embraced by squalls
by an oily & misshapen blinding"

ON SCORPIONS & SWALLOWS

Not claimed
by the accessible as contrast
or as competition by loss
or mathematic by peril

but occlusion as opposable phylums

minus a dark synesthesial as rote
minus the axial smoke of a rotted bonfire hamlet

I mean
oasis as savage dialectical rotation
meaning
species as aggressive salt
as curious vertical blazing

in reversed arrayal
I think of interior cobalt swallows
with predacious ignition

a contradictory igniting
beatific with scopolamine

like the withdrawn thirst of the scorpion
with its "five-segmented posterior"
with its "seven-segmented preabdomen"
with its sidereal tail ending in toxicity
"born alive"
active after darkness
culminate
with the fatal sting
of "Centruroides sculpturatus"

therefore
the birds & the ground dwellers mingle in my mind
like a magnitude of multiple nebulas
akin to "Synaceia"
or "Pterois"
or the lionfish
explicit with the power of fatality

so if I mine from the nebulas
these birds

these fish
these scorpions
I go blank
& seize vertigo
& gain a forthright diplopia

so when I look skyward
a doubled swallow seems to swarm
in a flock of endurance

& exhibits a verdet
an iridescent yellow tree
imbibing insects while in volation
with the reddish beak of the family of "Hurundinidae"
in flight
in their high migration houses
from boreal dawns in the north
to the Cape of Africa in the south

& so I make my imaginal leap
& connect the swallows in their height
to the "Red Jungle Fowl" anchored to terra firma
like the scorpion

with its neurotoxins
like "Buthus occitanus"
unlike the passeriforms
who exceed small birds in speed
not like the Labrador Duck
or the Carolina Parakeet
they exist
like the gaze
which renders the cliff swallows unevident
their withering thermal migrations
dialectically at odds
with electric living collectives

their mud jugs under ledges
less elaborate than the "ovenbird"
the latter's nest of inner spirals
with its one bubonic open door
opening & shutting
against the predatory sums of roving scorpion necrotics
this fiery movement across earth
then a galling guardian wolf

a guardian
creeping
carried at first on the back of the mother
then relentless
stalking
like the outsized "Panamanian ponerine" ant
"tearing its prey to bits"
or like the "digger wasp" injecting venom into the nerves

I then think
of the Wood louse
the Beach flea
the trap door spider

with the "simple small eyes"
transmitting figments
barely proficient at resolving a tincture
of compound stereopsis

then
the olfactory sight of the common ants of Formicidae
capable of aphid
herding

akin to the swallows
in terms of sphinxian insect singing

& the swallows
in flight across mesas
across the flank of exploding glacier tables
across a lake of random gravel fires

then the migrational zodiac
of the halos
of the helium winds
of the Lapse Rate in the atmosphere
& unlike the previous rocks
neither scorpion or swallow
condenses on any common finality
mingled at anti-vigesimal snappage
at pointless adrenaline breaking

their dialects erased
like a great flooded Playa
not equal
or mathematically orthomorphic
to any judgmental vector

they exist
oddly
like polyconic projections
never central to the fact
of a bare diurnal strategem

THE GHOST SURVIVOR

Body by drosera
by pure calliope as referent
as invaded mausoleum

the body then existing
as standing cinder under threat
condensed
brought back to the soil
as a sub-abandoned heresy
being a blue in-carnivorous thought arrangement
under an orange-white dust
next to a blank & verdigris spinning house

& this spinning house
brazen with tarantulas & probing
with its sun posts imploding
with its Macaws & adders as regressive sub-orders

the body in this haze
an apparitional ballast

a half form quaking
flowing through faceless compost arcana

calling out from jeopardous blindings
from disrupted falcons & armies
like salt without form
like general anthracite gone missing

THE NEWBORN

The newborn
as combat
as plesiosaur & yield
as listless momentary monster

ALIEN PERSONAS

Inside a squandered creosote hull
there exists a form of reptile optic
like a cold intrinsic sun
which advances through relentless interior offerings

the gulfs as bursts of mangers
of carnivorous pollutants
of intermittent personas
dissolving themselves
beyond each iota of reason

& so
those personas of the hull
committed to forms of alabaster summits
of shale
of riverine deceptions of labour

condensed
by a giant galactic carnivore
tied

to an oblivious stake of mercury
implanted in its heart
by a level of a-charisma
over & beyond the zodiac

THE POINTLESS NETHER PLOW

It is farming in an inclement sun system
like a powerless nether beast
fallen amidst random stellar debris

fruit changes form
light then quavers across distorted mural relics

the farmer then living as a clarified adder
his land forms compressed
his wheat suspended & flaring
his unstable forms
carving his soil with volcanic blue seeds

COMPRESSION & PURITY

In this fire of fluidic jeopardy
diamonds uncoil
& reconstruct & re-condense
like adjudicated burins
or telepathic moon forms

like psychic drafts & diacritics
being pressure by conundrum & purity
compressed below the level of the gaunt reflecting metals

diamonds
crushed & glinting pions
incessant suns in the pedalfer vapours
where the Sun quakes by quanta
by powerful interior fractal

the singular diamond
like a juggler or a hawk
in condensed mercator warrens
where signs ignite in the phosphenes

like the shape of a comet as Sedna
or holographic combustion
compressed
burning
the dialectic of the ice house

the ground as habitual day star
as aerolith
as perfect star in the fathoms
known as pyroxenes
as repetitious pyroclastics
as lowered concentrations of void
being basalt by subductive infinity

diamond as subduction
as errata of mist under vapour
& these diamonds in my mind
not of the human blood soil
of protracted avidity
but of blank alchemical stresses
being wealth as random mountain ore
being poetic spurs
being strange supraphysical hallucinatory hives

which come down & retreat in the ethers
like double blinded mountains
or a halting circuitous heat from the Permian or
Mississippian

not an avalanche of morals
or a decided human predicate
but the predicate as primordial
as helium
as olivine
as "hydrated minerals"
as feral ozone dosage

compression then
precocious
with neon reversals & flaring
with dense & angular heightening
being a fabulous schist
being monoxide & hearing
with the Sun spun around & condensed by petrology

THE DELUGE IN FORMATION

If one believes oneself as stasis
there exists no seepage
no neural density or scar

one then saturates as ash
as pointless cannibal's lethargy
as dislodged ink from a podium or a treatise

one comes to know de-mobility as a craft
as an ark which solders itself to specifics

yet to know one's non-sequestered through mundane
advancement as doorway
or basic habit as speculation

I am speaking of chastisement
or cross-referential super-imposition

within this condition
I am more like a crow from crucial underwater fires
a crucial underwater crow

neither Chinese or Shinto
but of the black dimensionality as hidden underwater mass

which persists by daring
which seems at the surface
a purposeless kinetic
or a pointless Mandrill's infection

saying such
I consider myself a reddish Shinto crow
then just as strongly
a black anathema crow

then just as quickly
a sun fed crow from snow washed volcanoes

so I look to myself as winter
as inclement carrion monger
as flight through great electrical haze

I being blur who shapes the empyrean
who invokes withdrawal
who instills in his forces stunning psychic transference

COMBUSTION & LEAKAGE

FOR CESAR VALLEJO

Brooding on life, brooding
slowly on the strength of the torrent
——CESAR VALLEJO

I ascribe to you combustive ozone & witness
a-rhythmic triune inferno
acidic soil & self-leakage

your legacy
being assault by tragic torrent
like a courier compounded in a blizzard of whispers

being random synapse structure
being blood which seems to gain on itself by over all despair
by its subject of dismissive errata

these remain its crucibles
its rocks
its discursive embitterment

one then smells its flanks
its chiaroscuro of bottoms

& because your blight obstructs
your words break off & scatter
inside their schizophrenic mazes
consoling themselves
by means of the fleeting
the brutal

pained as you spoke
about the shadows accrued between tumbleweed & slaughter
between occlusion & its riots
you sat breeding
multiple & varied as a ghost

Cesar
it was you who dug bread
for the miners & the burros

knowing full well the tungsten & its threading
knowing full well its metallic underground peninsula
swinging back & forth
between hunger & the motion of its 3 solid bodies
collapsing in the dust
with its oxides soaked by instantaneous compounding

& you knew this compounding by superior reason
by proletarian contaminate
by charismatic striation

events were empowered by residue
by pointless tension
by motionless combat as advance

then grammar as voltage
by infernal slippage
by illuminate ellipse
enriching the mind by defanged advancement
by fatigue of place
by malarial disclosure

being perpetual solar force
or telepathic culture
being lunar force by diacritical osmosis
curiously decoded
as working sawdust invictas
as brooding voice by specificity

I am speaking here of your disrupted seasons
speaking with Lorca in nomadic transpicuity
with Artaud in fleeting glimpses
your life obscured by anesthetic linkage
by broken luck & betrayal

I am listening to the salt inside your hunger
like an emaciated grail
corroding second after second your haunted porous urn
the self of your self wasting on blood counts
its disaster
its molecular ruination
haranguing itself
with the body ill fitted & emerging with new deficits

yet with a new engrained astonishment
which rises up as language
which unsettles strength with derangement
knowing the monads disperse
through a medium
not quite glass
not quite poison

not quite the power of a prone or visible galaxy
an enigmatic heresy

a surge through ailing verbal fauna
like a burned monomial wool forming into blisters
into suns which extract the metaphysical from mystery
& it was by this grace
you called on Marx
on Feuerbach
on Hegel

you described descriptive neural banter
as partial centigrade rotation
like ammoniated refuse setting fire to the skin

this was your workbook Cesar
precipitous with pressure
with logarithmics as jeopardy

you were the body which dwelled inside a Yokahama seaquake
from which birds broke loose as ammoniated spells

then the tellurian opposition of the simplistic hyrax
or the terse dysfunctional serval
parallel & cunning by indifferent roulette

the vivacity then stunning
like the memory as aural parasite
as stained but provocative ambrosia

of course your poetry quakes with dialogics
with personal scarring on its corpses
with scrawling literal tincture as battle
which persists at rebellious pacing

it continues to know in the present the Hadean splinters
the variable eye in its blindness
being a warped & contagious recognition

so when your brooding went astray
it further increased your wrath
your spellbound naumachia struggling out of stone
akin to Soutine with inner gallstone etching

I think about the early loss of love
the bogus jailing in Trujillo
your residue from fallible personal exhaustives

again
the splintered Catholic agenda
the derived in-tendency from the hearth
allowing your view of the parochial tome
as a misplaced inferno

of course
you lived in an unknown furnace
as a wasted forensic salt count
as domestic abutment
as feral living arrangement

you fed on harassment
you took in coded peasant's sugar

living on caffeine
on a factual kind of pumice

there was always about you
this alien kindling
this speculation as dread

you were the immaculate saboteur
the incognito footman
your auric fumes
partially illumined by furtive candelabra

I can think of nothing less than incendiary deepening
than precocious enciphering
being the call & response of ailing falcons & sea hares

your irrational range
true suffering as flamboyance
as starving carnivore as disappearance

as result
your ghost no longer casts image

like ether in silk
or an echo within an elevated mayhem

your territory:
vehement
your self-gambling:
panic

you took risks against deception
against abduction & bitterness
always encountering
a swamp of locusts in the phosphenes

you remain for me
the introvert
hidden with cattle
with proletarian morale

at times
your voice
extinguished in the chronicles
exchanged in the fauna of your wayward measuring sands

calling up vacuums written in vicuna
through fabulous confounding
through anarchical visceral cascade
like unstructured findings
curiously filtered
through a partially constricted gullet

you who called on the deafness of God
on secretive personal ascension
with the fleas shorn from your hide
as you propounded to the end
the fuels in your fiendish mineral ballistics

in the end Vallejo
your weight
your attenuated positrons
fighting for every inch of ground
for every coding in the trachea
seeming to condense
as a bedlam of study
or a curious momentary eel
ensconced with a scarred Newtonian floating

HORIZON AS PARALLEL & SONAR

The horizon scrawls itself as interior distillation
as interminate terminology
as floating ocular ravine

it remains
a parallel radiophony
a flashing sun in phantom waters
being aquatic flame in exhaustive sonar kingdoms

like ejected sonar feathers
parallel & subsumed
being a phantom turned around in itself
like a sudden or repetitious unfoldment
like the colour in pointless carrion reversals
neither parallel or verdigris
its greenish photon layers
its spark by decohesion
like an urn inside a droplet
flashing at the pole of decohesive tenor

a sun form flashing as itinerant decohesion
like a ghostly ibis which dissolves as flame from interior nebulas

a splayed meandering flame
a parallel anointment
a sun which subjectively incinerates

the horizon being mist
& lines of summa
& blank imaginary braille

clandestine inferno
the sudden inferno of braille

being dark mercator current
being heavenly Pyla dune

seismological monsoon
epicentral sea

or glass or refraction from an epicentral fault scarp
its sounds splayed as perfect Sonoran suns
as heatless & vanished calliopes

as systems of systems
as suns turned around inside suns

each horizon in Serpens
being mists & forms asleep on Canopus

like hypabyssal fragments
or moth schematics
or light from collective hydrology

the horizon
being a mock sun
an image of a sun
sometimes white
sometimes pointlessly parallel as mirage

or
mathematic mercator brewing at curious limit

being a droplet
a phantom
a terminated water

a cosmic sabbatical projection
a cosmic tributary ore
a flowing ocular petrology

so if the horizon be petrology
or strictly terminus as gale
it cannot claim its drift
as seismic non-projection across specific planetary ore

or perhaps
a sabotaged or subtractive geometrical schismatics

perhaps horizon in a sea flowing basin
blurred
seemingly infecund
where light erupts from phantom underwater graves
like a blank subductive sigil
or an irregular or soundless migratory shift
being a ground unmarked by invisible detonation

perhaps
horizon as fabulous underwater hive

as strange cylindrical erosion
expelling leptons
& fabulums
& kingdoms of dust as detachments

& these detachments
like glacial fire in hanging valleys
or pointless views from formless dromedary angles

the horizon being the Sun in the pointless dromedary system
in its immaculate reduction
in its waters which divide

being the Sun as interior radium
as echo or moth on Callisto
as focus or droplet on Rhea

being the ammonia in the Sun as immaculate voltage & ether
as powerful parallel & drowning

& this drowning
unlike the craft of the serpent

or the bird reversing flight by its embers
this is light by darkened lateral flame
by curious & parallel osmosis

thus
the human form at the horizon
plowing at "civil twilight"
doubly blind & co-planar
continuing by strange deficience

his blank vehicular anomaly
a combustive assonance
a tourmaline invicta subsumed by the horizon

being mist as combustive tourmaline
as compressed or fragmented atlas

the world as mist
as disrupted planar debate
being a blaze with double polar moons
being fiery positrons as land

the dawn then ablaze
as circumstantial drought
as polar devastation
circling in the dunes
as a rarefied mist or atlas

a menace
a star which gathers as ferocious simulation
as sub-deducted writhing pond
being a circumpolar Fahrenheit which spins

which complicates
its centigrade as momentum
like a cipher on Ceres
alive with its seasonal & subterranean deflection

so the Sun on Ceres
being an ice house inferno
a pointless teeming arroyo
its orbital blaze like flowing insular buttes

& these insular buttes through greyish aural soil
like a strange lenticular mass

haunted as a zone of wafting tributary ponds
of deflected tributary ponds
opening & closing as isoclinal respiration

& I am not speaking of sudden medial moraine
or cultivated fog by disaster
but of horizon as droplet
as volcanic cinder
of floating furnace as schism

being tautology as mica & schist
as water in a boatless fever warren

the horizon
part detraction
part powers from a fractious hydrogen well

so the horizon & the Sun as fractious hydrogen misnomers
as spells
as sorcery
as hydrography as furnace

being the insular dharma of rocks
being hydrogen forms spinning diamonds in the earth
being power at galvanic twilight

germination then spawned as sonic vascular blinding
as Sun inflamed earth
being horizon as solstitial invasive

like a formless neon spark
or formless argon concentrations
being nebular hologram as hive
through deafening oil as concentration

THE COSMOS AS FRAGMENT

a bell in a grotto
a sun with its flame
riveted inside a selva

WATER ON NEW MARS

"Being water
I am the voltage of rocks
of algid suns in transition
flying across a scape
of bitter Martian dioxide

moving boulders by abandoned fossil premonition
the poles quaking
the Sun misjudged through my aperture of prisms

my oceans pre-existent
& trembling as a soil inside iridium constellations
like invisible glacial misnomers
like dark magnetic rivers
strange & totemic with current

where proto-jaguars advance
where lichen de-exists
where the cells blaze at the cusp of a hovering fahrenheit

having evolved from space
my perfect first falling
like an indigo amniotic
burrowing like a blank encrypted gravitas
as wandering anaemia
as floating proto-quanta
obscuring my own deafness
where the winds howl
where the soil maladjusts to my thinking

it is a 100,000,000 years before my coming
I use no exterior crafting to withstand me
no nautical monology to sculpt my various geometries
to claim & disclaim my pointless hydrogen summas

I remain the greenish sonar heron
the combustible yeast
the exhausted locust's hull
pre-enzymic with the force of hydrated complication
itinerant with visitation
my voice seeming to spin from the great Quetzal palace in space

like diamonds falling from a fabulum of ciphers
like a river of moons flowing over slate

I
who extract from my powers a blizzard of orbits
I
who know from my powers a portion 90 x 9 a billion times
over

of course this is grace by sumptuous hesitation
by delimited decimals as impedition
of ferocious power imploded by displacement
by seething hydrogen as osmosis

I fall by terrible quickening in darkness
creating an unstable balance as weather
as dissonant inner functioning as power

at 3/4 cycle I regress to implosion
so as to ignite each shift through ascensional quandry

so that levels shift & return
through exponential draft
through meteoritic harvest

seeming to probe by insatiable regression
by limitless rudiment
by a stunning pluvial osmosis

water as sigil
as carnivorous land fields gone blind

this is New Mars
its mountain heights blackened
like the doubled seeing of Olympus Mons
with its sinister scars
with its deflected rays from Phobos

New Mars
a smaller or faultless deafness
alive
through ghostly silhouette
through kinetic margin as dissension

I exist as its rigour
not quite riddle
not quite seismic
being gnomic
being neural innuendo
as polar argon as ascendant

all of the above
a phantom botany
empowered by a curious technical width

& this botany
transmuted above the separable waters
above the patterns which foment the planet as noxious exhibit

this is the density
at which I scatter
& de-reveal my own essence as other than bi-pedal
as other than a sternum with warped occipital range

I am presence with the speed of a strange electrical horse
with the vertical force of a transmundane stampede

so that I form in this range of sound
with the land of New Mars
as explorational blankness

a blankness
which burns
& extends
& accelerates
& goes beyond a toneless pause as its counting
as separable glyph
as purely ocular holograph
which vibrates as ratio pouring law over sand

I am the presence of water on New Mars
not the Mars of observation
with its regimented molecules
but the Mars co-tested by a powerful telepathy

I have arrived on New Mars
before the Sun was gathered as carbon
before its moons were reduced to abstemious laterality

my motion
splintered suns as telepathy
with my polar magnetics blue
my inter-galactic gullies incessant
prior to the planes
where my presence pre-existed
as baffling cellular symbol
as Akashic cuneiform & carbon

on New Mars
the Sun will double rise on 2 planes
will flash in the northern embers
will dispel on the southern grounds
the pale light blue with its carnivorous torrent
with its double moons as Phobos by molecules
as Demos by articulate cipher

on Phobos I am blizzard as gene
I am transmuted grain

moons which live like Sedna or Pluto
self-heated like dwarfs

I remain on New Mars as a great lenticular hail
as a pluperfect hail
divided & sub-dominant without visage
knowing the ferocious axial canyons
knowing the brutish dust of their darkness
with their surface obscured with trans-rendered cinders

this being my proto-water as it flowed a billion years ago as rills
as forms of pre-destined amphibics

I as water
which exists as centripetal centigrade
as strange philosophical hydraulics
not as frayed or osteological disadvantage
as astro-paleontology
as spores which fall from the plasma of space

as aesthetic photon orchids
as utopian jaguar contagions

as if
my rainbows were understood as photonic desecration

or shapeless fumatory plankton
akin to a whirlwind of falling starfish from heaven

& perhaps on Earth
I'd be transfixed to the fact of a composite creature
perhaps a falcon
a lion
a crocodile
& a whale

a fertilizing prana
a fore-guarded analogy

having throughout my duration
a fore-knowledge
of harmonian astral lakes
of supernatural green isles
knowing that purity compresses as primal mobility
that its waters blaze as instantaneous nomadics

again
I stress presence as imperfect lunar cryptography

as point beyond resistance
as dialectical self-waning

I weave
from the mists surrounding Phobos
vibratic echos beyond Saturn
knowing the purification beyond spoils
beyond the memoir of entropy
becoming a great triangular neon sail
on an astral frigate
on Mayan bark as lacunae

flying with Neptunian cormorants
with composite snow forms as wasps

as presence
I am of compound feeding
being sonar in fabulous solar nurseries
where hidden suns transpose from my presence

I create an animate visual ether
where light evolves
where blazing takes form as a proton-proton emission

perhaps
I am water on New Mars
in a strange acanthus canyon
where infinity is scattered as reversed ascensional trailings

knowing the ice winds that gather at the various poles
perhaps Rhea or Europa
knowing the central pole
the auric pole
which fleets as quantum flame beyond the asteroids

thus
I am water as alternate nitrogen sand
as scorched & shifting profundity

I am other
in a spinning neutron bay
being mirage & illusive with blinding

on New Mars
I am transmogrification
I am hypnos
I am buried spell in iridium

being fumatory soil in nigrido
as divinatory ashes from the sea

a disjunctive nitrogen
with its waves compressed & black
like cold imaginary scrawling
fulminate with a kind of ether as fish
igniting the ghosts of cells as an epic

no pre-preparation
no rational or balanced criteria

on Earth
I am the crystal bird as ointment
listening to itself according to dictates scattered across a nebula
further back in time than the Permian or Ordovician

perhaps I am the current with the transmuted cells
with the riveted ocular thirst
non-aligned to magnification
to listless & dominating lateral equilibria

because
in the lesser scale or dimension
New Mars remains sienna
with two imploded moons
circling with utmost vacuum as thunder

this doubled Mars
focused as strabismus
as purified eclectics
like the sulfur which roams in the Columbia Hills

the plateaus
like a glyph of wayward trilobites
which waver like the pull from irregular errata

my presence
being that primordial mineral flaring
that calligraphy which en-scars by pauses & flamings

a tumultuous scarring
like a quake from tumultuous kelvins
where the moons coalesce in waves
like burned or ellipsed volcanoes

such is the case of indefinite ruination
by ferment by withdrawal
where suns collapse & renew
& continue to de-exist

these being the figments where fauna commences
water being a quaking aural infinity
being a porous crystal in the flatlands
or an isometric crag in the Andes

this being Earth
& Mars
& New Mars
& being

this being a fabulous hydro-concision
like burning ice & marks
as imaginary ice steps on Rhea

which combines in blinding human ascendance
as thermotropism or touch
or the mind erupting from a pointless cortical breech

as trans-ocular ruin
I am astonishing spectre
a coursing solar day as darkness
baring boreal roots as proto-sorghum through spectra

to this degree a faultless thermal conjuration
a sightless phlogiston feeding
knowing doubled lightning bends
which flow in Sirenum Fossae

a blaze across a violet vascular field
a velocity alive in carbon astral water

being spell as blind electrical osmosis
being arc as ravine & chasm

New Mars
a blind & meandering energy as conundrum
as a magnetic platelet
minus itself in particles
being a glossary in Martian inaudia

where a partial sun expands
being a fabulatory vector
trans-active with vicinity"

ON ANTI-BIOGRAPHY

For me, biography is a lantern, burning in the midst of parenthetical opaqueness. In a sense, it is a ruse, a phantasmic meandering, brighter or dimmer, according to the ecletic happenstance of terror.

Me, I've been sired in anomaly, in an imagery of brewing grenadine riddles, a parallel poesis spawned from curious seismographic molten. I say curious, because the original stalking arc has disappeared into the wilderness of an a priori blizzard, which gives birth to a level, like a portal of fire conjoined with the lightning field of mystery. I call it the poetic guardian dove, the hieratic alien wing.

It is the non-local field, the non-particle acid, flowing into my cognitive iodine rays, into the vicious fires of my tarantella marshes. So I dance with vibration, with the solar arc spinning backward around the miraculous force of a double green horizon. Simultaneously, I escape the territorial, while remaining within the burning loops of my own momentary seizures, guarded by ferns, legs plowing land, the face and the mind guided by stars.

So, I am a martyr of drills, of spates of specific lingual flooding, casting at times, a mist or a mirage, like a caravan of yaks, transporting tungsten and water. Conversely, to give a graph of dates, to single out a bevy of personal social lesions, would invert me, would turn me around a diurnal bundle of glass, staggered, with a less than fiery temperature, partially nulling my sensitivity to falling phonemic peppers, to the inclination towards victory which burns in the dawn above heaven. For me, this is the green locale, the pleroma of eternal solar essence, glinting, full of fabulous maelstrom diamonds, an empowered hegira of drift, of claustrophobic rainbow spectrums which empty themselves, and return to themselves, like having an image go out and return to itself, so that it's power transmutes by the very energy of its looping; and I think of myself, the poet sending signals into mystery, and having them return to me with oneiric wings and spirals, so much so, that I forget my prosaic locale with its stultifying anchors, with its familial dotage and image reports, with its dates inscribed in trapezoidal feces. I am only concerned with simultaneity and height, with rays of monomial kindling, guiding the neo-cortex through ravens, into the ecstasy of x-rays and blackness.

MY INTERIOR VITA

I was born under Leo, under its signpost of heat, and what has evolved from such coloration is a verbal momentum always magnetized to the uranic. A verbal rhythm prone to the upper hamlets of starlight, my predilection being instinctively honed to the fluidic motion of the sidereal. This is not to say that the protean aspects of Earth cease to amaze me, or cease to enthrall me with its natural magic. The winds, the bays, the deserts, ceaseless in my mind like a teeming field of Flamingo flowers, or a sun-charged clepsydra. Yet above all, the earth being for me the specificity of Africa, as revealed by Diop, and Jackson, and Van Sertima, and its electrical scent in the writings of Damas.

Because of this purview I have never been drawn to provincial description, or to the quiescent chemistry of a condensed domestic horizon. I've always been prone to exploring the larger scope of predominant mental criteria as exhibited by the influential civilizations over the span of time which we name as history. For instance, within the Roman or American criteria I see the active involvement of what is called the left brain and its natural gravitation towards separating life by means of active fragmentation. Yet at a more ancient remove there exists the example of Nubia and Kemet unconcerned with life as secular confiscation, but with the unification of disciplines, such as astronomy, mathematics, philosophy, law, as paths to the revelation of the self. Knowledge then, as alchemical operation, rather than an isolated expertise. So when various knowledges fuse in my writings, insights occur, revealing an inward light whose source is simultaneous with the riveting connection between flashes of lightning.

For me, language, by its very operation, is alchemical, mesmeric, totalic in the way that it condenses and at the same time proves capable of leaping the boundaries of genre. Be it the drama, the poem, the essay, the novel, language operates at a level of concentration modulated by the necessity of the character or the circumstance which is speaking. My feeling is that language is capable of creating shifts in the human neural field, capable of transmuting behaviours and judgments. Humans conduct themselves through language, and, when the latter transmutes, the human transmutes. The advertisers know this linkage, but to a superficial degree, so when language is mined at a more seminal depth of poetic strata, chance can take on a more lasting significance. And I do not mean in a didactic manner, but in the way that osmosis transpires, allowing one to see areas of reality that heretofore had remained elided or obscured. I'm speaking here of an organic imaginal level which rises far beyond the narrow perspective of up and down, or left side and right side, which is the mind working in the service of mechanical reaction. Rather, I am thinking of magnetic savor, allowing the mind to live at a pitch far beyond the garish modes of the quotidian. One's life then begins to expand into the quality of nuance naturally superseding a bleak statistical diorama.

I was always drawn to realms outside the normal reaches of comment even at an early age. I would sustain imaginary dialogues with myself by continuously creating imaginal characters very specific in their cryptic ability to spur continuous inward rotation. Imaginal kings, warriors, athletes, angels, always igniting my mind with their ability to overcome limits, to sustain themselves beyond the confines of normal fatigue. And it was during this period that I had my first confrontation with a spectre. It spoke to me in the dead of night, commanding me to rise from my bed and follow its presence into I know not where. I remained frozen as it spoke to me, and as I vividly recall I could utter no sound. I knew I was not dreaming, because as I stared into the darkness its strange niveous image formed in my vision, and took on for those unbelievable moments a staggering animation. Of course I was not believed the next day when I reported my contact to my mother. And years later she could never recall me recording the incident or my reaction to the incident, something totally out of character for her. Nevertheless it confirmed for me the activity of the supra-physical world which has remained with me in all my subsequent moments. Thus the rational world has never been able to annul my alacrity for what the mechanically-sighted call the invisible.

This reality was further strengthened when first hearing the recordings of Eric Dolphy and John Coltrane. It was during my early teens and listening to the music was absolutely electric. It made me feel that I had allies, that there were others who knew that the material world was completely permeable, and that none of the rationally stated boundaries could contain the imaginal. Of course all of this happened before I knew anything of poetry. Yet I was already in the poetic, the music already opening me up to creativity linked as it is to the inner and outer plane. The inner burst of creative power and its circulation in the world on an international scale. Eric Dolphy in Berlin, John Coltrane in Antibes, Cecil Taylor at Moosham Castle in Austria, Duke Ellington in Dakar. So by the time I read a book on Rimbaud some seven years later I felt a definite relation between his inner experience and my own. Close to finishing the book I found myself writing my first poem, and I immediately felt a great liberty transpire within me, a liberty which suddenly flashed to creative fruition.

And I've found over time that this liberty continuously burns, and is capable of transmuting all that it touches. I've found no discipline which is foreign to it. Architecture, politics, mathematics, mysticism, all prone to a higher verbal kindling, to a different archery of usage. This is not to say that poetry serves as a didactic device, no, but as a magical instrument with the prowess to overcome the mortality of the temporal. It is fiesta outside the limits of the measured diurnal regime where the constraints of the conscious mind vanish without trace. So by the time I discovered Surrealism and the writings of Artaud, Cesaire, Breton, Lamantia, and Bob Kaufman, I felt ripe for exploring the subconscious levels of the mind. Then connecting the power of such writing with Sri Aurobindo's supra-conscious mind, the Tibetan Book of the Dead, and the Egyptian connective between visible and invisible domains, I was able to develop within an instinctive motif of linguistic arousal. And as was for Cesaire earlier, the Surrealism opened me up to animate use of language not unlike the ancient African atmosphere of consciousness. Life being an unbroken motion of consciousness, poetry is for me the celebration of that unbrokenness.

Creativity being an ongoing praxis, is a continuous trance, in which one deals with the unification of worlds, rather than fostering inclement fragments. Insights, worlds within worlds, which include not only scintillations of the conscious mind, but more importantly, its ability to both elevate and descend, thereby traversing the triple levels of the mind, the conscious, the supra-conscious, and the sub-conscious minds, creating in the process a concert of worlds.

THE POPE AT AVIGNON

"I remain the Pope at Avignon

because nothing in this world can conceal me

I test the limits of my evil

prone as I am to bloody offspring by debacle

I

being the leathery witness of evil

I

being the culture of the offspring of evil

I

who ferry toxins on the Sabbath

I

who blossom by means of spillage & errata

seek in his conclusives to amalgamate hypocrisy

to ascribe to force a plain & turbulent bleeding

assured that my own hosannas resound

that the force of my name alters cataracts in hell

because

I can in no ways do otherwise

perhaps pontificate

announce bread

breed the scars on my flanks as signs

from the above

raising as I do certain virgins up from hell

extracting a carnal medicine from the eyelids

I left Rome

to inculcate the Bosporus

thus I remain strategic

in that my eyes are flawed

that my hands are tragically spent

this

the charismatic occurrence

of I who seem to dwell within the pastures

of deeper sweltering

I

being the sorcerer who shreds gowns

who creates justice in life by supreme

& opulent verdict

by miasma which lingers & verifies confusion

by the dark forms of sand

by the diamonds which erupt eros

that would lead one to believe that I am

clinging to ruination

for inconsolable payment

for making land conform to the object of rent wheat

thus

I am posterior to different forms which inhale the Sun

thus

I am recondite by instability

having fathered 2 magnetic serpents

in my struggle with containment

of course I am divided

merismatic & melancholic

thus

I grant myself the folly

the ambrosia

the scales that weigh cunning in my mitre

thus

I trespass heaven

& ascend through stars through nucleic transposition

thus

the bishops advance my meddlesome fornication

one by one advancing my secrets

absorbing a tacit henbane in the skin

& one by one they'll fail

as if a medley of serpents conspired against

their treason

& when they die

I'll give them over to God

I'll say that they posses a cleansed rooting

& an ochre foil in their hearts

I'll say that their secret assignations were justified by limit

by double fathering in the genes

so that their offspring will conspire

to teach me consummation

to take in the soils from amniotic shelters

with codes which reveal the lower constituency

of boasting

I am a miracle in this regard

I control by lamentation

by fragments & disbelief

by feral conundrum as status

thus

I co-habit on sheets of coal

because

each contaminate strengthens

as if I pulled a fetid sheaf from lagoons

& traded various boats of opal

along with a cardinal or reddish manganese

& so

amidst the routes of the Bosporus they admit

my own accursedness

yet they shield me

they offer intrigue

they offer forgone specifics

so as to shelter my mission

knowing as they know

that gold condenses as evil

that Jesus Christ limits & is sorcerous & askew

they know

Kemetic investigation

they know

the stolen urns

the non-recorded labour

they know

that the one true God has never emended his thinking

or struggled with his own catharsis

understanding that I've slept with the offspring of eels

I've hidden a lamb in my garments

having struggled with beasts & all the 4 legged raptors

thus

I've come to my decision

to slaughter as opposed to retainment

always

concocting in my brain

the structure & physiology of monsters"

VIBRATION FROM THE COAST OF INDIA

One feels its harried anodyne vultures
its populace of rats
its vexing by bubonics

the fact
that the body is eaten as vapour
as base invisibility
to be discarded
to be rinsed
with carking polonium & lime

so there are basics
intrinsically freed of themselves
of their dark extrinsic imperial patterns
as if the holocaust body had never existed

never peaking at fruition
as claw
or model
or fabric

as to fate

& its ultimate de-existence

there remains

a galactic brewing formation

never weighed by the cells

or by measures invented

by an onerous grasping of sorghum or principle

BEGINNING AFTER-EXISTENCE

On the threshing floor

there are spiders which astonish

with replications which irradiate

which strike resistance

which terrify

which de-foil carnivorous amoebas

with each fiber

with each mandible

with each blood knot gone astray

flailing

embryonic

shifting

out of red or exerted magma

threading their weight

throughout a melanotic angle

into ghostly osmosis

A ZODIACAL INSTANT

To co-ordinate tigers

to look into the bright domain of sullen

de-activity

is to walk on threads

is to hallucinate navamshas

AMIDST THE LIMINAL

In the cranial foundation

there are colours which erupt

into a blankness which reconnoiters

which re-erupts into ratio

into earthquake curricula

in which a form of flames spirals

frayed at its core by potentia

ANOTHER PLANE

Absorbing a tumbled foci

absorbing verdurous angularities

with blackened electron resistance

with a coiled & perfidious complication

like a fowl in a blazeless solar ocean

scattering its sound

across noiseless sodium rejoinders

COMPOUND HIBERNATION

Those who glance about me
who cease to see inside the Sun
who cease to imagine its destabilized pre-quanta
cannot know me
cannot know my ethos as pumice
as mingled apparition or flare

my perception through the prior sun that I ingest
like a blackened pre-existence
or collected hawks through assignation

the Sun
with its dualisms
with its pre-biotic photons which waver

perhaps
9 suns before the Sun existed
before the oceans seemed formed
there were molecular drafts

akashic precursors
floating proto-ammonia

I think of carbon
& wisps
& floodings

of feral combat shelter
where blank geometry accrues

before separable biology was born
before the contradictory ballast of de-existent protozoa

being scorching photon by abstentia
like a pre-atomic sigil
destabilized as blizzard

a pre-cognitive rotation
a strange galvanics of the cosmos

& because of this galvanics
one reeks of invisible tremor
walking around in league with daunting helium affliction

thus
the mirrors in my skin like haunted salamander fluid
like cells bereft with cooling centigrade rotation

therefore
I know the abyss as volatile lunar transposition
as sub-liminal mantis as climbing
as splintering

therefore I am not
an oily or blasphemous yogin
collapsing in default by sudden anger or water

yet I am compound
struggling with scattered mental a-rhythmia
with partial psychic aphasia
intensive
illusive
aloof by interior compounding

COPING PRANA

It is the way I breathe
through chronic terrifying ferns
through a black ungracious stoma

it is this uranium rejoinder
this impact pointing backwards

& when witnessed
causes observers to panic
to blur
& forget
& to flee

they can't see my approach
my wayward dorsal looming
my lettering in black drizzle

it is my approach
my weaving
my sigil as curved embankment

therefore
I can never name myself
or plot myself
according to the sparks or the splinters from the work bench

dazed
ruthless with salivation
with my awkward insular roamings
I am like a few darkened eaglets riveted against the moon

then I am brought to a table by deafness
feasting with herons
which spins me by embranglement
by in-circular abatement
always seeking to have me neutered beneath my derma
so as to talk to myself
so as to cancel my structureless scrutiny

they speak of me as lawless
as despicable
as a typhoon in a sea well
as to morals
as to fixed & accelerated combination

they fix me
as deserted
bereft
as a fragment from a starving lion's compendium

I am considered
as pointless positron without image
as hieroglyph
as sundial
as martyr

being leakage from a barbarous index province

The state of the world calls out for poetry
to save it. LAWRENCE FERLINGHETTI

CITY LIGHTS SPOTLIGHT SHINES A LIGHT ON THE WEALTH
OF INNOVATIVE AMERICAN POETRY BEING WRITTEN TODAY.
WE PUBLISH ACCOMPLISHED FIGURES KNOWN IN THE
POETRY COMMUNITY AS WELL AS YOUNG EMERGING POETS,
USING THE CULTURAL VISIBILITY OF CITY LIGHTS TO BRING
THEIR WORK TO A WIDER AUDIENCE. IN DOING SO, WE ALSO
HOPE TO DRAW ATTENTION TO THOSE SMALL PRESSES
PUBLISHING SUCH AUTHORS. WITH CITY LIGHTS SPOTLIGHT,
WE WILL MAINTAIN OUR STANDARD OF INNOVATION AND
INCLUSIVENESS BY PUBLISHING HIGHLY ORIGINAL POETRY
FROM ACROSS THE CULTURAL SPECTRUM, REFLECTING
OUR LONGSTANDING COMMITMENT TO THIS MOST
ANCIENT AND STUBBORNLY ENDURING FORM OF ART.

CITY LIGHTS SPOTLIGHT

1

Norma Cole, *Where Shadows Will:*
Selected Poems 1988-2008

2

Anselm Berrigan, *Free Cell*

3

Andrew Joron, *Trance Archive:*
New and Selected Poems

4

Cedar Sigo, *Stranger in Town*

5

Will Alexander, *Compression & Purity*

6

Micah Ballard, *Waifs and Strays*

7

Julian Talamantez Brolaski, *Advice for Lovers*